ABC Book of Affirmations for Melanated Kids
Vol 1: Real African Kings & Queens

By Tapiwa Dzingai

sunrize

ABC Book of Affirmations for CONFIDENT KIDS
Vol. 1: Real African Kings & Queens

Published by Saanrize Ventures LLC
1023 East Hyde Park Blvd
Chicago, Illinois
60615

Copyright© 2022 by Saanrize Ventures LLC

All rights reserved. No portion of this book may be reproduced or distributed in any form and in any translation or by any means, electronic or mechanical, including photocopying, recording, or by any information storage and retrieval system, without permission from the publisher, except as permitted by U.S copyright law.

If you would like permission to use material from the book (other than for review purposes), please contact permissions@saanrize.com

ABC Book of Affirmations for Confident Kids is available for purchase at special quantity discounts for bulk purchase for sales promotions, fundraising and educational needs.
For details, write to: wholesale@saanrize.com

Creator: Tapiwa Dzingai

Cover Illustrator: Marvin Opuni Kwabia
Book Designer: Chané Isaacs
Illustrators: 14 Black Illustrators* from all over the world

*All artists are fully credited in the Acknowledgments

ISBN#: 978-1-957130-04-0
First Edition, 2022

Thank you. Siyabonga. Tatenda for supporting our mission to "Unlock the Inner Royalty in Every Child!"

www.confidentkidsseries.com

To the little royals reading this book,

I wish for you what I wish for my two girls and my son —
my heartbeats and the motivation behind this book.

May this book remind you that you are beautiful, you matter, and you are capable of greatness.

May it help you fall in love with who you are and spark your curiosity and pride in Africa and African heritage.

May these characters bring you joy and broaden what you think it means to be a beautiful prince or a princess.

May this help you see each other as the "little Kings and Queens" that you rightfully are.

Most importantly, I hope this book brings you together and inspires you to be the empathetic "little royals" that this world needs more of.

Created with love, passion, and purpose.

Tapiwa Dzingai

(Mai Matidaishe, Anashe & Simbarashe)

I am Adventurous!

A is for Adventurous

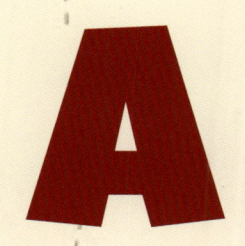

like Mansa (King) Abubakari II, Voyager King of the Mali Empire.

He was a ruler of an Empire with power and duty,
But he longed for adventure and to discover the world's beauty.
He wanted to sail the seas in hopes of finding new land,
So he gave up all that power to explore the world so grand!
He set sail with a huge fleet and thousands of men,
Not knowing if they would find anything, but then...
They landed in the Americas! They were happy indeed.
And this was hundreds of years before Christopher Columbus sailed the seas.

The world is your oyster. Don't be afraid to go out on adventures!

I am Beautiful!

B is for Beautiful

like Queen Tiye & King Amenhotep III of the Kingdom of Kemet.

Queen Tiye was very beautiful, the prettiest woman in all the land.
She was confident, intelligent, and oh so grand.
She was one of the most powerful queens of her time.
Her beauty radiated from within and was simply sublime.

King Amenhotep III was such a great King you will be hard-pressed to find an equivalent.
It's no wonder they called him "The Great" King Amenhotep III or "The Magnificent."
His beauty from within shined so bright.
When he ruled Kemet, it was so peaceful, rich, and full of light.
He was kind and friendly, always good and never bad,
Making the time that he ruled one of the best the kingdom ever had.

No matter what you look like, never ever doubt: you, too, are extremely beautiful, both inside and out.

I am Creative!

C is for Creative

like Queen Moremi of the Kingdom of Ife.

Queen Moremi was very clever and became a secret spy
Who went undercover to find her enemies' secrets, but she had to be sly.
Unafraid and innovative, the African queen used wisdom,
Took a risk for her people and, because of that, she gave them freedom.
She used the information she gathered to craft a plan to help set her people free.
Her statue now stands in Nigeria for everyone to see.
It's called the Moremi Statue of Liberty, and it's the tallest in the land.
At forty-two feet high, she will forever stand tall and grand.

All of your challenges have solutions. Just believe in yourself, and you will find them!

I am Daring!

D is for Daring

like Pharaoh Queen Hatshepsut of the Kingdom of Kemet.

Queen Hatshepsut was a trailblazer and she dared to be different.
As one of Kemet's longest-reigning female pharaohs, she was magnificent.
A female pharaoh, yes that's right!
Strong, brave, and full of ideas so bright.
I bet you didn't know they had those, too,
And she was so good at her job, so committed through and through.
She was determined to make her time as queen useful throughout
And made sure she left Kemet a much better place, without a doubt.
So when someone says, "Tell me something I don't know!"
You can say, "Hatshepsut is the name of the longest-ruling female pharaoh."

You, too, can be anything you want to be. Don't let anything hold you back.

I am Exceptional!

E is for Exceptional

like <u>Gaspar Yanga</u> of Veracruz, New Spain.

Gasper Yanga was born an African prince, but was sadly captured as a slave and carried to New Spain.
He grew up and led a successful rebellion, one of the first in the Americas domain.
He led this group of free slaves to Pico de Orizaba,
the highest mountain they could climb,
And built a place of safety for other runaway slaves all in good time.
A safe colony for Black people is what he established and wanted to see,
One of the first places in the Americas where enslaved Black people could be safe and free.
Spain tried to bring Yanga's people back under their rule,
But he led his people and defeated Spain in a victorious duel.
Yanga is highly admired and is now known as a national hero,
And there are statues of him in many cities in Mexico.

You are capable! You are powerful! There is no limit to what you can do.

I am Fearless!

F is for Fearless

like Kandake (Queen) Amanirenas of the Kingdom of Kush.

The Romans had just defeated the Egyptians, and they would not quit.
They now wanted the Kingdom of Kush, but Queen Amanirenas would not allow it.
She knew her army was much smaller, so she led a surprise attack
And captured their three cities, but they still fought back.
Years of battle followed, and one time she injured her eye,
But once it healed, she got back up, continuing to fight and try.
They finally defeated the Romans, and Amanirenas bathed in victory.
Thanks to her bravery and leadership, the Kingdom of Kush was free.

You can be afraid and do it anyway. Fearlessly go after your BIGGEST dreams

I am Generous!

G is for Generous

like Sultan Saifuddin Firuz Shah, the second African ruler of Bengal.

He was a wise and compassionate king
Known for the generosity he would always bring.
He was incredibly kind and gave plenty to the poor all the time,
But many did not approve of this and thought it was such a crime.
They were worried they would run out of money with how much he gave away,
And they tried to get him to listen to what they had to say.
But when Sultan heard how much he was giving he threw his head back and laughed.
He told them to double it and learn to not be so greedy and daft.

You will get more happiness from giving more, not getting more. So give freely without ever expecting anything in return.

I am Honorable!

H is for Honorable

like King Shamba Bolongongo of the Kuba Kingdom.

Known as the African "King of Peace," he used his power for the good of his people.
He made sure to always treat everyone in the kingdom fairly and like his equal.
He allowed both men and women to be leaders of the land,
And he hated war so much that he declared it officially banned!
It's no wonder that he was so widely admired.
He was just the type of king everyone desired.

Try to be honorable in all you do. It's more precious than riches or fame.

I am Incredible!

I is for Incredible

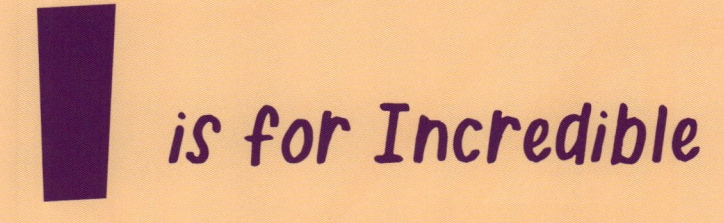

like <u>Lozikeyi Dlodlo</u>, Queen of the Ndebele Kingdom.

Lozikeyi was a very bold and remarkable queen.
One day her husband, King Lobengula, disappeared mysteriously, nowhere to be seen!
Lozikeyi stepped up to the plate and took on the challenge to lead the kingdom.
She brought her people together and helped spark Zimbabwe's fight for freedom.
She was independent and diligent, a natural-born leader indeed,
Using her smarts and insight so her kingdom would always succeed.
It may have been many years since the remarkable Lozikeyi left this earth,
But she will always be remembered for her bold spirit, value, and worth.

Love the awesome and amazing person that is you.

I am Joyful!

J is for Joyful

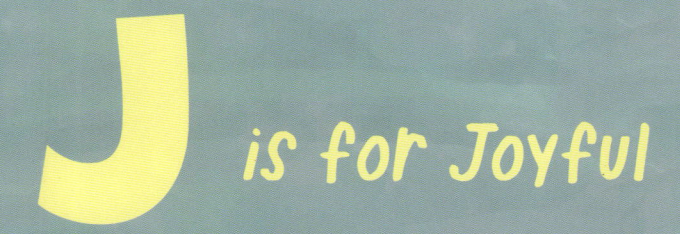

like King Ezana of the Kingdom of Axum.

Ezana was a great king, making sure his people were happy and fulfilled.
He was kind and worked hard, and for that, they were thrilled.
"May this please the people" was engraved on every coin across the land,
And he even shared his wealth with the people he conquered, so they could live happily hand in hand.
Ezana made Axum a peaceful place and with all the joy he would bring,
It's no wonder he turned out to be their favorite king!

Choose to spread joy. Be so happy that when others see you they feel happy too.

I am kind!

K is for Kind

like King Moshoeshoe I, founder of the Sotho Kingdom.

He took his people to the Butha-Buthe Mountains and settled them there.
He gave land, protection, and refuge to many who ran from the war and needed care,
Uniting them as one to form the Basotho nation.
He embodied the spirit of "ubuntu," showing others humanity and compassion.
Together they built the great Kingdom of Lesotho, and it was oh so grand.
He was kind to his neighbors, and his actions earned him respect all over the land.

Kindness costs nothing but means so much. Choose to be kind.

I am a Leader!

L is for Leader

like Queen <u>Ndate</u> Yalla Mbodj of the Waalo Kingdom.

She became queen of the kingdom when her sister no longer could
And faced attacks from many, but strong and determined, she still stood.
She led her small army of men and women in the fight to protect her land,
Defeated the French, and led the Senegal war of resistance firsthand.
She was a strong and brave leader and the last queen of the Waalo Kingdom,
Remembered as one of the most powerful, always fighting for her people's freedom.

Be the kind of leader you would want to follow.

I am Magnificent!

M is for Magnificent

like Queen Tassi Hangbé of the Kingdom of Dahomey.

She had a twin brother who was the king, but sadly, he passed away.
So she disguised herself as him and led her army without a moment's delay.
The people admired and respected her for her leadership and wisdom
And crowned her the queen of Dahomey, as she proved well equipped to guide the kingdom.
She chose all the women to be her loyal guards, increased their power and their duty,
And formed the first elite army of all women called the "Agoodjié."

Whatever challenges you come across each day, you have the power to overcome them.

Beaufort Sea
Chukchi Sea
Bering Sea
Gulf of Alaska
Aleutian Islands
Alaska (U.S.)
BROOKS RANGE
ALASKA RANGE
RUSSIA
CANADA
Hudson Bay
Labrador Sea
Baffin Bay
Davis Strait
QUEEN ELIZABETH ISLANDS
VICTORIA ISLAND
ROCKY MOUNTAINS
GREAT PLAINS
NORTH PACIFIC OCEAN
NORTH ATLANT OCEAN
UNITED STATES
GREAT BASIN
COLORADO PLATEAU
APPALACHIAN MTS.
SIERRA NEVADA
Ottawa
Washington
Gulf of Mexico
MEXICO
BAJA CALIFORNIA
Tropic of Cancer (23°26′N)
CUBA
THE BAHAMAS
JAMAICA
HAITI
DOMINICAN REPUBLIC
BELIZE
HONDURAS
EL SALVADOR
NICARAGUA
COSTA RICA
PANAMA
Caribbean Sea
VENEZUELA
COLOMBIA
GUYANA
SURINAME
French Guiana
ECUADOR
Equator (0°)
BRAZIL
PERU
BOLIVIA
PARAGUAY
CHILE
ARGENTINA
URUGUAY
ANDES
MATO GROSSO PLATEAU
ATACAMA DESERT
GRAN CHACO
PAMPAS
PATAGONIA
French Polynesia (FRANCE)
Tuamotu Archipelago
Austral Islands
SOUTH PACIFIC OCEAN

Greenland Sea
Norwegian Sea
Barents Sea
Kara Sea
Laptev Sea
ICELAND
NORWAY
SWEDEN
FINLAND
RUSSIA
North Sea
UNITED KINGDOM
IRELAND
GERMANY
POLAND
BELARUS
UKRAINE
FRANCE
Bay of Biscay
SPAIN
PORTUGAL
ITALY
ROMANIA
GREECE
TURKEY
Black Sea
Caspian Sea
KAZAKHSTAN
MONGOLIA
UZBEKISTAN
TURKMENISTAN
AFGHANISTAN
PAKISTAN
IRAN
IRAQ
SYRIA
JORDAN
SAUDI ARABIA
YEMEN
OMAN
Mediterranean Sea
Red Sea
Arabian Sea
Bay of Bengal
INDIA
CHIN
MOROCCO
ALGERIA
LIBYA
EGYPT
CHAD
SUDAN
SOUTH SUDAN
ETHIOPIA
SOMALIA
MALI
NIGERIA
CENTRAL AFRICAN REPUBLIC
CAMEROON
GABON
Gulf of Guinea
DEMOCRATIC REPUBLIC OF THE CONGO
UGANDA
KENYA
TANZANIA
ANGOLA
ZAMBIA
ZIMBABWE
MOZAMBIQUE
NAMIBIA
BOTSWANA
SOUTH AFRICA
MADAGASCAR
SEYCHELLES
MALDIVES
SOUTH ATLANTIC OCEAN
INDIAN OCEAN
French Southern and Antarctic Lands

Antarctica

Mansa (King) Abubakari II	14th Century AD	Mali Empire	Mali, Senegal, the Gambia, Guinea, Niger, Nigeria, Chad, Mauritania, and Burkina Faso
Queen Tiye & King Amenhotep III	14th Century BC	Kingdom of Kemet	Egypt
Queen Moremi	12th Century	Kingdom of Ife	Nigeria
Pharaoh Queen Hatshepsut	15th Century BC	Kingdom of Kemet	Egypt
King Gaspar Yanga	17th Century AD	Veracruz, New Spain	Mexico
Kandake (Queen) Amanirenas	1st Century BC	Kingdom of Kush	Sudan and South Sudan
Sultan Saifuddin Firuz Shah	15th Century AD	Bengal	Bangladesh and India
King Shamba Balongogo	16th Century AD	Kuba Kingdom	Democratic Republic of Congo
Queen Lozikeyi Dlodlo	20th Century AD	Ndebele Kingdom	Zimbabwe
King Ezana	4th Century AD	Kingdom of Axum	Eritrea and Ethiopia
King Moshoeshoe I	19th Century AD	Sotho Kingdom	Lesotho
Queen Ndaté Yalla Mbodj	19th Century AD	Waalo Kingdom	Senegal
Queen Tassi Hangbé	18th Century AD	Kingdom of Dahomey	Benin

ARCTIC OCEAN
ARCTIC OCEAN
ARCTIC OCEAN
Greenland
(DENMARK)
ICELAND
NORWAY
SWEDEN
FINLAND
RUSSIA
IRELAND
UNITED KINGDOM
DENMARK
EST.
LAT.
LITH.
BELARUS
POLAND
GERMANY
FRANCE
UKRAINE
ROMANIA
ITALY
SPAIN
PORTUGAL
GREECE
BULGARIA
Black Sea
GEORGIA
TURKEY
KAZAKHSTAN
MONGOLIA
CHINA
NORTH ATLANTIC OCEAN
MOROCCO
ALGERIA
TUNISIA
LIBYA
EGYPT
SYRIA
IRAQ
IRAN
JORDAN
SAUDI ARABIA
KUWAIT
UNITED ARAB EMIRATES
OMAN
YEMEN
TURKMENISTAN
UZBEKISTAN
KYRGYZSTAN
TAJIKISTAN
AFGHANISTAN
Islamabad
PAKISTAN
NEPAL
BHUTAN
INDIA
BANGLADESH
BURMA
LAOS
THAILAND
VIETNAM
CAMBODIA
South Ch Sea
Bay of Bengal
Arabian Sea
SRI LANKA
MALDIVES
MALAYSIA
BRUNEI
INDO
Western Sahara
MAURITANIA
MALI
NIGER
CHAD
SUDAN
ERITREA
DJIBOUTI
SENEGAL
THE GAMBIA
GUINEA-BISSAU
GUINEA
SIERRA LEONE
LIBERIA
CÔTE D'IVOIRE
BURKINA FASO
GHANA
TOGO
BENIN
NIGERIA
CAMEROON
CENTRAL AFRICAN REPUBLIC
SOUTH SUDAN
ETHIOPIA
SOMALIA
UGANDA
KENYA
GABON
REP. OF THE CONGO
DEMOCRATIC REPUBLIC OF THE CONGO
ANGOLA
TANZANIA
ZAMBIA
MALAWI
MOZAMBIQUE
ZIMBABWE
NAMIBIA
BOTSWANA
LESOTHO
SWAZILAND
SOUTH AFRICA
MADAGASCAR
SEYCHELLES
INDIAN OCEAN
SOUTH ATLANTIC OCEAN
THE BAHAMAS
CUBA
DOMINICAN REPUBLIC
JAMAICA
HAITI
Caribbean Sea
PANAMA
VENEZUELA
GUYANA
SURINAME
French Guiana
COLOMBIA
ECUADOR
PERU
BRAZIL
BOLIVIA
PARAGUAY
CHILE
URUGUAY
ARGENTINA

GLOSSARY

Adventurous
willing to try new things, ideas, or experiences.

Creative
explore possibilities and new ideas.

Daring
brave, courageous.

Exceptional
remarkable, outstanding, special.

Generous
show kindness to others, willing to share with others, more than what is expected.

Honorable
worthy of respect, have a good name because of their good deeds or behavior e.g. honesty.

Incredible
amazing, impressive, awesome, wonderful.

Magnificent
impressive, brilliant, superb.

Innovative
new ideas or ways of solving a problem.

Committed
focused or dedicated to finish something.

Slave
someone who is forced to work for someone for free and is not allowed to quit and live freely.

Pharaoh
name given to both male and female rulers and religious leaders of Kemet (ancient Egypt).

Humanity
being caring, kind, thoughtful and sympathetic towards others.

Sublime
extraordinarily beautiful and grand.

Trailbrazer
someone who leads the way for others to follow.

VISUAL GLOSSARY

Prosthesis

Artificial device designed to replace a missing human part (from birth, or due to an accident or health problem) or help the body work better.

Down Syndrome

Condition that affects the way a child's brain and body grows, leading to physical and learning delays and sometimes even some distinct facial features e.g. slanting eyes, small chin, round ears and flattened nose.

Alopecia

Condition that causes some some kids and adults to lose their hair on the scalp and sometimes other places on the body.

Albinism

Condition that some people are born with, that causes them to have less melanin in their skin, hair, and eyes and be more sensitive to the sun.

There are over 2,000 languages spoken in Africa. These are just a few examples of how to say King or Queen in a few of the native African languages spoken on the continent.

LANGUAGE	KING	QUEEN
chichewa	mfumu	mfumukazi
hausa	sarki	sarauniya
lingala	mokonzi	mokonzi mwasi
shona	mambo	mambokadzi
somali	boqor	bogorad
swahili	mfalme	malkia
twi	ɔhene	ɔhemmaa
xhosa	ukumkani	ukumkanikazi
yoruba	oba	olori
zulu	inkosi	nkosikazi

THANK YOU!
SIYABONGA!
TATENDA!

to all 15 of these Black artists that trusted and sowed into the vision of this project to unlock the inner royalty in every child. I am so grateful, privileged, and honored to have collaborated with you to bring the "Confident Kids Series" to life.

And I can't forget my hubby, Brian and my children, close family and friends for their incredible support and sacrifice over the past two years to help bring this vision to fruition. And a special thank to my daughters, Marley (6y/o) & Zoe (4 y/o) who also served as the lead artistic and editorial directors for this project. As much as this series is my gift to the next generation and the world, it has been an incredible gift of healing and I am thankful and humbled for all of your unwavering support and guidance to make it possible.

Thank You!

ACKNOWLEDGEMENTS

Cover Illustration
Marvin Opuni Kwabia
Ghana

Adventurous
Kelly Wanjira Kinyua
Kenya

Beautiful
Aaliayah Haynes
Barbados

Creative
Ockiya Cliff Omiebi
Nigeria

Daring
Salma Shokry Mohamed
Egypt

Exceptional
Bre'Anna Washington
U.S.A

Fearless
Karen Bravo
Colombia/Australia

Generous
Baba Aminu Mustapha
Nigeria

Honorable
Axel Massa Mavounzi
France

Incredible
Mudiwa Marasa
Zimbabwe

Joyful
Michael Mwangi
Kenya

Kind
Ashley McKenny
U.S.A

Leader
Draya Abrams
U.S.A

Magnificent
Ken Ahossan
Benin

Book Designer
Chané Isaacs
South Africa

Also available in the series

See all books in series at
confidentkidsseries.com

Follow us on:
◉ @confidentkidsseries
ⓕ @confidentkidsseries